Tiling and Mosaics

in a weekend

Tiling and Mosaics

in a weekend

Deena Beverley

BETTERWAY BOOKS

CINCINNATI, OHIO

For Daisy. Thank you for demonstrating grout mixing and general apprentice skills, friendship and tolerance well in excess of your tender years.

Acknowledgments

As well as providing the photography that illustrates the finished projects, I would like to thank Andrew for his treatment of the step-by-step techniques photography. His practical approach has produced pictures that describe the making of the projects succinctly and enticingly.

I would also like to thank Anna Sanderson for giving me the opportunity to explore this subject in such a varied way, for her invaluable early contributions to the project concepts, and for her restrained, yet quietly encouraging, approach during the production of this book.

Heartfelt thanks to Karen Hemingway of Murdoch Books, with whom I first made the contact that led to the writing of this book, and who waited patiently as my working on it threatened to overwhelm all other projects in its path.

Finally, thank you to my husband and daughter for sharing my total immersion in this project with such good humor, enthusiasm, and excessive reserves of stamina.

Distributed to the trade and art markets in North America in 2002 by
Betterway Books
an imprint of F&W Publications, Inc.
4700 East Galbraith Road
Cincinnati, OH 45236
(800) 289-0963

Copyright © 1999 Murdoch Books UK Ltd

ISBN 1-55870-616-X

A catalog record for this book is available from the Library of Congress.

Editor: Geraldine Christy
Designer: Sue Miller
Photographer: Andrew Newton-Cox
Stylist: Deena Beverley
Template illustrations: King & King
Commissioning Editor: Anna Sanderson

Color separation by Bright Arts, Hong Kong
Printed in Singapore by Tien Wah Press

Contents

Introduction

Tiling and mosaics have enjoyed a massive resurgence of popularity in recent times. Certainly mosaic items and tile makeovers are among the most requested and well-received projects for home-improvement magazines and television programs.

One of the most frequently asked questions is "How can I cover up my hideous tiles?" That is why a high proportion of this book has been devoted to revamping existing tiled surfaces. The suggestions given are intended to be just that. Let your imagination run wild, and use the basic techniques and suggested materials as starting points to transform your own tile nightmares into exciting new decorating schemes.

Tile paints have improved dramatically in recent years. As long as you clean and condition the tiles thoroughly, following the manufacturer's directions to the letter, there is no reason for painted tiles to look second rate. As with most decorating projects, preparation, as dull as it may be, is the key to success.

Also, consider the grout as being as important as the tiles in your makeover schemes. Although it is technically possible to clean grout and paint straight over it at the same time as the tiles, it can look horribly amateurish. It is advisable to steer clear of grout-renovating products that promise instant results. Follow the suggestion given in the Mediterranean color-washed tile project, and rake out the surface of the old grout and start again. Tiles look best offset by fresh-looking, matte grout in a complementary color.

The information given for grouting tiles applies equally to the mosaic projects as to the tile projects. After all, mosaic projects are just tiling projects using smaller tiles. To clear up any confusion you may have regarding the difference between the words "tiles" and "tesserae"—there isn't any! Tesserae has become a generally accepted term used to describe the individual components of any mosaic.

Now that mosaic is so popular, many stores are selling mosaic supplies, but they may be uninformed about their applications. In contrast, specialized mosaic suppliers, however friendly, can be somewhat overwhelming with their in-depth knowledge of their craft. To ease your learning curve, here is all you need to know about mosaic in a nutshell. There are two basic mosaic working methods: direct and indirect.

Direct is where tesserae are applied directly onto a surface. It is the simplest, most satisfying way to work, and is used throughout this book.

Indirect refers to the method where tesserae are applied to a backing sheet, then inverted onto a surface. This enables mosaicists to work away from the site, for example when working on a large, exterior project. Another application of the indirect method is when an absolutely flat surface is required, but the precise uniformity of the results can be disappointingly soulless.

For the direct working method used here, apply tesserae rippled side down. Ceramic, vitreous, and metallic tesserae are essentially all the same thing: small, flat, machine-made square tiles that are generally halved and quartered with nippers. The colors and texture are what differentiates them. Smalti are handmade tiles that are often used in the self-grouting method; that is, just pushed into adhesive or grout, which then rises up to surround each one.

Mosaic is a medium that is infinitely variable according to your own tastes and the amount of time and effort you wish to expend. These projects should give you a taste of the exciting possibilities afforded by this most satisfying of crafts.

Deena Beverley

Mediterranean color-washed tiles

Your existing plain machine-made tiles can attain an expensive-looking, hand-painted finish. Bring a touch of Mediterranean rusticity to them with a simple color-washed effect.

This tiled wall suffered from two problems. First, the undulating surface, in a room with little natural light, looked permanently dingy—white without light on it merely looks gray! Second, the grout had seen better days, and was unappealingly grubby, with or without the effects of light.

Handmade and painted Mediterranean tiles are universally admired for their rich, glowing tones and depth of color. Choose a warm palette of closely related subtle earth shades to produce a folksy, homey look. Now the light hitting the ripples in the tiles has something to play with, and reveals the many layers of color built up by repeated color washing. Each layer is a shade slightly different from the one beneath, which gives added interest to the surface.

This technique could be applied to any tile, not just white. However, it would be a good idea to blank out any really hideously distracting color in white, or better still, ivory-colored tile paint before you begin building up your beautiful translucent glazes. They would not look nearly as effective on a turquoise or avocado base!

Although colored grout is available, the color palette available now is so restricted that it is well worth making your own by simply coloring the water with which the powder grout is mixed by using universal stains or acrylic paint.

Planning your time

DAY ONE
AM: Rake out old grout; clean and condition tiles; paint on first coat of glaze to all tiles

PM: Paint on subsequent coats of glaze; varnish

DAY TWO
AM: Grout

Tools and materials

Grout-removing tool

Ceramic paints, cleaner-conditioner, glaze, and varnish (use same brand for compatability)

Paintbrushes

Powder grout in natural buff color and PVA adhesive

Paper towels (for cleaning tiles)

Clean cloths

Wooden tongue depressors or tile squeegee

Disposable mixing bowls for grout (such as clean food containers)

Aluminum foil

Tile or old plate to use as palette

Day One

Step 1
Rake out old grout using a grout-removing tool.

Step 2
Thoroughly clean and condition the tiles using a product of the same brand as the paints. Follow the manufacturer's directions precisely for best results.

Step 3
On a foil-covered plate or tile, dilute ceramic paint with the glaze so that it produces a translucent, colored mixture. Using foil enables you to change the color frequently without having to stop and clean the palette each time.

Step 4
Paint on the glaze with a brush to leave deliberate brush marks in one direction only. Continue to paint the tiles to produce a random effect. Leave one or two in their original colors. Vary the direction of the brush marks from tile to tile for an authentic, handcrafted appearance to the walls.

Step 5
Mix small quantities of additional colored glaze to produce closely related toning shades. Brush these on top of the colors when the first color is dry. Allow to dry.

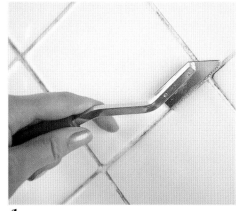

1

2

3

4

5

6

8

Step 6

Add several coats of varnish, allowing each coat to dry thoroughly before applying the next. Allow to set fully overnight.

Day Two

Step 7

Color water with red and burnt umber universal stains or acrylic paint. Add PVA adhesive in a ratio of approximately 1 part PVA to 5 parts water. Mix this with the powder grout. Aim for a dryish, mud-pie consistency.

Step 8

Apply grout with a wooden tongue depressor or tile squeegee and spread evenly, taking care to push it well down into the gaps between the tiles. Remove excess gently with a soft cloth. Allow to dry thoroughly.

7

Pebble mosaic floor

Interspersing terra-cotta tiles with pebble mosaic makes an unusual decorative patio feature. This project would also make a charming floor surface for a summerhouse or sunroom.

Most gardens have an area that could use a little hard flooring, but concrete slabs are just too awful to contemplate. Special handmade exterior flooring surfaces look great, but can prove expensive over a large area. This pebble mosaic solution borrows from an age-old tradition of using pebbles for abstract and pictorial effects. The result is inexpensive, surprisingly simple to achieve, and looks equally at home in town or country gardens.

It is important to prepare the groundwork well before you begin. Although you want a striking textural finish, aim to have the tops of the pebbles exactly level with the surface of the tiles so that the floor is even and comfortable to walk on. You do not want a surface that causes garden furniture to wobble irritatingly, so take care to level the dry mix before you place the pebbles in it, and take equal care to push all the pebbles in to leave a uniform height.

Contrary to what seems a natural way of working, the pebbles in pebble mosaic are not simply laid lengthwise on the surface of the dry mix, but are pushed down into it vertically, for maximum strength. As you work, you will quickly become accustomed to selecting pebbles for their size and appearance when viewed from the end.

Please do not take pebbles from beaches without checking with the local authority. Legitimately collected pebbles, conveniently graded according to size, are available inexpensively from specialty suppliers, who can often deliver heavy loads and provide invaluable advice and help with preparing your individual base prior to commencing the decorative part of the work. If you have an existing unsightly paved area you could also consider removing alternate slabs, and filling in the gaps with pebble mosaic.

Planning your time

DAY ONE
AM: Prepare site

PM: Lay concrete

DAY TWO
AM: Make and spread dry mix; plan final design

PM: Add pebble and tile mosaic; brush on dry mix; sprinkle with water; protect until cured

Tools and materials

Bucket and shovel

Cement

Coarse sand

¾" (20 mm) aggregate

Watering can with rose

Burlap

Plastic sheeting

Trowel

Piece of 4 x 1" (100 x 25mm) board as straightedge

Pebbles—large, medium, and small

Frostproof terra-cotta tiles

Hand brush

Day One

Step 1

Prepare a 2–3" (5–7.5cm) thick concrete base 4" (10cm) below what will become the finished ground level. Use a mix of 1 part cement, 2 parts coarse sand, and 3 parts aggregate. Allow to dry overnight, covered with damp burlap to prevent too rapid of curing during dry weather, or add dry burlap/plastic sheeting to protect against frost in winter if you live in a cold climate.

Day Two

Step 2

Prepare mortar dry mix. Mix 3 parts coarse sand to 1 part cement—leave dry, do not add water.

Step 3

Pour dry mix onto the concrete base and smooth flat, using a straightedge. The base should be the thickness of the tiles below ground level.

Step 4

Construct the main pebble motif by pushing pebbles vertically into the dry mix so that they protrude to a height equal to the thickness of the tiles. Make sure the height is uniform.

Step 5

Bed terra-cotta tiles onto the dry mix, using a slight wiggling motion for good adhesion.

Ready-made dry mix

It is possible to buy bags of pre-mixed concrete and mortar that contain the right proportions of each ingredient; this saves you the trouble of having to calculate ratios.

1

2

3

4

5

8

6

7

Step 6
Place additional pebbles to fill in the rest of the design.

Step 7
Brush dry mix evenly over the surface to fill any gaps, then sprinkle the whole area with water. The dry mix will absorb the water and begin to harden over the following few days.

Step 8
Cover with burlap or plastic sheeting supported by a board so as not to touch the mosaic surface until the mortar has completely cured (about a week). Avoid walking on the area if possible for three weeks or so.

Painted fabric tiles

Give your kitchen tiles a more homey look with painted patchwork motifs. Copy scraps of fabric from elsewhere in your decorating scheme for a coordinated look.

P lain, large-sized tiles are a popular and practical choice for kitchens, but large areas of them can look clinical and cold. Hand painting existing tiles that are sound but uninspiring sometimes seems daunting, but this project uses a stamping technique to produce neat, infinitely repeatable results in record time. A few deft brush strokes to highlight the floral elements of the design gives a laboriously hand-painted feel without actually being labor intensive.

This design takes the colorful painterly fabric of the curtains as its inspiration, but you could restrict yourself to any one of the stamping techniques shown in the instructions for an equally effective result. The gingham motif, in particular, would work well scaled up onto a bigger stamp for even faster results.

Whatever you decide, do not skip the initial stage of painting brush strokes in a color that is almost the same as the color of the tile. The process may seem boring, but the slight difference in tone beneath the stamped motifs is what gives an overall warm effect of painted fabric rather than cold, glazed tile. The naive, open pattern created by the sponge also looks more comfortable over a broken-color ground than on harsh white.

If you are using this project to revamp existing tiles that are not an obliging white or ivory, simply blank out their color with neutral-colored tile primer and tile paint before you begin to add the patterns.

Planning your time

DAY ONE
AM: Clean and condition tiles, then mask grout and surrounding area; apply ground color and mark off patchwork "pieces"; cut out sponge shapes; stamp on; apply polka dots

PM: Apply gingham and checked motifs; add leaf and flower detail

DAY TWO
AM: Add "stitch lines"; remove pencil marks

PM: Varnish

Tools and materials

Cold-set ceramic paints, cleaner-conditioner, and satin varnish (use same brand for compatibility)

Stiff-bristled flat paintbrush

Fine paintbrush

Lighter fluid

Aluminum foil

Tile or old plate for palette

Expandable sponge (from craft stores)

Quilting tape (narrow masking tape sold in fabric stores)

Masking tape

Ballpoint pen

Cotton swabs

Wooden skewers

Small scissors

Ruler

Pencil

Thin cardboard

Ceramic outliner in dark color to tone with color scheme

Day One

Step 1
Prepare the tiles using cleaner-conditioner, following the manufacturer's directions precisely.

Step 2
Mask off grout with quilting tape to preserve the visual contrast between the matte grout and the slight sheen of the finished tiles. (If you want a really speedy result, simply omit this stage and brush over the entire surface, grout and all.) Mask off the surrounding area with standard-width masking tape to protect against overpainting.

Step 3
Brush cream-colored ceramic paint over the tiles, leaving deliberate brush marks in one direction only. Allow the base color of the tile to show through.

Step 4
Using a ruler and pencil, lightly mark out the tiles into smaller rectangles and triangles to mimic patchwork pieces.

Step 5
Draw simple leaf and flower shapes on an expandable sponge with a ballpoint pen. Cut out the shapes using small scissors. Place them in water so that the sponge expands.

1

2

3

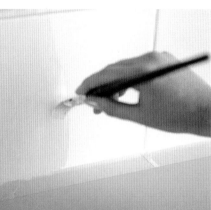

4

5

6

Step 6

Dab the sponge flower shape into a foil-covered plate or tile to pick up a minimal amount of ceramic paint. Holding a piece of thin cardboard to shield the marked-off edge of a patchwork "piece," stamp flower motifs onto a random number of patchwork pieces.

Step 7

Apply leaf motifs in the same way. Make sure that the motifs "break" the edge of the patchwork pieces visually for a realistic printed fabric effect.

7

Using stiff-bristled brushes

Really cheap, stiff brushes are perfect for some of the brush painting in this project, which actually requires visible brush marks that allow the base color to show through. Their stiffness also means that they pick up and hold very little paint, making it easy to apply just a thin coat.

Step 8

Using a sliver of sponge, bend it between your fingers as you stamp on the flower stems, to produce natural-looking curves.

Step 9

Dip a cotton swab into a small amount of paint to produce polka dots. As with the flowers and leaves, apply dots that seem to disappear between the "seams" of the patchwork pieces for a fabric-like effect.

Step 10

Cut small squares from the expandable sponge. Insert a wooden skewer into the sponge to form a handle. To form the gingham motif, paint rows of squares, leaving a gap roughly the same size as the piece of sponge between each one.

Step 11

Mix a color that is 50 percent lighter in tone than the first color of the gingham design. Stamp in between the rows of existing squares to complete the motif.

Step 12

Using a barely loaded, stiff-bristled flat brush, paint a loose, checked design onto some of the remaining "pieces."

Using colored grout

For a really vibrant look, replace dingy grout with brightly colored grout before starting to decorate the tiles. Just add color to the mixing water with universal stains or acrylic paint.

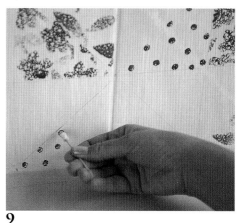

8

9

10

11

12

13

15

14

Step 13

Using a fine paintbrush, add a few lines of a darker color than the flower and leaf motifs for added visual emphasis. Keep the lines free and spontaneous.

Day Two

Step 14

Using a ceramic outliner in a dark, toning color, paint on "stitch lines" close to the edge of some of the tiles to mimic running stitch, cross stitch, and oversewing. Allow to dry thoroughly. Remove any visible pencil lines with lighter fluid on a cotton swab, using a gentle sweeping motion.

Step 15

Apply several coats of satin finish ceramic varnish, allowing each coat to dry thoroughly before applying the next. Remove the masking tape.

Gingham bath panel

Freshen up your bathroom with this crisp gingham-influenced design for a bath panel. It utilizes reject tiles and is a satisfyingly fast-growing project.

Planning your time

DAY ONE
AM: Plan design; mark bath panel; cut tiles

PM: Clean, scuff, and seal bath panel; apply white tiles; apply border tiles

DAY TWO
AM: Grout

Tools and materials

Tile cutter

Tiles—white, light blue, dark blue

White waterproof tile adhesive

Powder grout in natural buff color and waterproof PVA adhesive

Brush for applying PVA

Goggles and protective gloves

Notched trowel

Scuffing tool (nails driven through piece of scrap wood)

Tile nippers

Tape measure

Pencil

Straightedge

Cloths for grouting

Colored pencils

Graph paper

Bath panels are generally not seen as the most exciting aspect of a bathroom scheme, which can be a mistake. This fresh gingham design can easily be translated into any colored check to suit your own decor and will definitely create an impact. The only point to remember when choosing colors is to make the paler tone roughly 50 percent lighter than the darker tone. If the difference in tone is too great, the fabric feel will be lost. Here a blue chambray colored tile with a speckled texture and matte finish has been used to give a cottony feel, which works well with

dark blue. Most machine-made colored tiles are available in a matte finish as well as the more usual gloss. Ask your tile supplier for details.

Larger tiles are used for the bulk of the panel. The remaining, checked design makes good use of a tile cutter to transform a few boxes of standard plain-colored reject tiles into homemade tesserae.

Cutting the rounded edges off all the tiles gives them a crisp, square edge and an authentic mosaic look. However, you could simply apply uncut plain white tiles to the main part of the panel and finish with a single border of the checkerboard design if you want a faster result.

Here a buff-colored grout replaces the usual white. It is every bit as important to consider grout color carefully as it is to choose tile color. The grout delineates the tiles and should serve to emphasize their color and placement. White grout tends to dominate visually and somehow leaches color from the surrounding tiles. The natural color here also picks up on the styling of the room, which has a Shaker feel, and prevents the mosaic from looking too cold and clinical. Use extra tiles to trim mirrors and other accessories to match.

Day One

Step 1
Experiment with the design on paper until you achieve a design that will work both visually and physically for the size of the panel; remember to allow for grout widths in all your calculations.

Step 2
Measure and draw the design onto the bath panel, dividing the dimensions to give the sizes to which the tiles will need to be cut.

Step 3
Cut large squares of white tile to size using a tile cutter. Cut border tiles into strips ready for nipping into smaller squares.

Step 4
Wearing goggles and protective gloves, use nippers to cut the border tile strips into squares and place each different color into a separate container.

Step 5
Clean, then scuff, the bath panel to provide a key, or rough surface, for the tile adhesive.

1

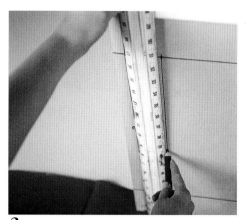

2

3

4

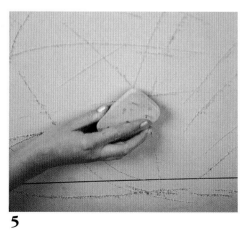

5

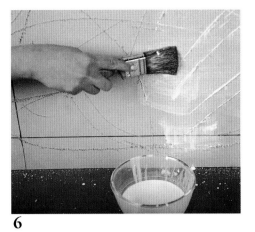

6

7

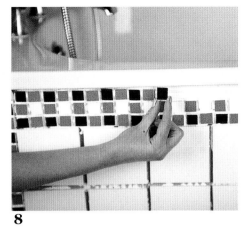

8

9

Step 6
Seal the scuffed surface with a solution of 1 part waterproof PVA and 1 part water.

Step 7
Apply tile adhesive to the backs of the large white tiles using a notched trowel and press into place using a slight twisting motion. Use offcuts of white tile trimmed to the border width to support the tiles while the adhesive starts to set.

Step 8
Apply tile adhesive to the border area a little at a time and press in the trimmed tesserae in the correct order to form the pattern you designed in Step 1. Allow to set overnight.

Day Two

Step 9
Mix buff-colored grout powder with water that has had waterproof PVA added in a ratio of roughly 1 part PVA to 5 parts water. With a sponge or cloths, and with the grout mixed fairly dry and stiff, work the grout into the joints using a circular motion. Polish any grout from the face of the tiles with a clean cloth to finish.

Alternative checks

For an even faster project, tile the main part of the panel with white tiles and finish with a border of tiles printed or painted in a gingham design.

Garden tool box

Store all those bits and pieces of garden paraphernalia that otherwise seem to end up on the floor of the garden shed in this quirkily decorative cupboard.

An old wall-mounted cupboard is transformed into a useful garden storage area; perhaps for all those smaller, fussy items such as pruners and plant ties seem to become easily displaced in the average crowded shed.

Many of us find old garden tools quite irresistible. This project utilizes inexpensive junk-shop finds in this charming mosaic of found objects, which also includes the rim and base sections of tiny terra-cotta pots.

Grouting such a myriad collection of shapes and sizes is painstaking work, almost requiring the meticulous care involved in an archeological dig. As you rub away the grout to reveal the keys and tile shards lurking beneath, you must be careful not to take the level of the grout down so far as to reveal the tile adhesive, yet you need to uncover every lovingly applied mosaic piece.

By using a combined tile adhesive/grout product applied thickly, and simply pushing the pieces into place, the project could effectively be completed as the mosaic is constructed, without the need for separate grouting. However, a separately applied grout unifies and smooths the delineations between the mosaic pieces so pleasingly that I recommend the more labor-intensive option without hesitation.

Planning your time

DAY ONE
AM: Cut bases off pots; plan design; scuff and seal cupboard front; nip pot shards and rims into smaller pieces

PM: Apply adhesive to cupboard front and apply mosaic

DAY TWO
AM: Grout; remove excess with scouring pad

Tools and materials

Wall-mounted cupboard with recessed door

Old terra-cotta pots

Tile saw

Miniature terra-cotta pots (from florist's supplier)

Old keys and old hand fork

Scuffing tool (nails driven through piece of scrap wood)

PVA adhesive

Paintbrush

Pebbles

Scouring pads

Dark gray frostproof powder grout

Waterproof tile adhesive

Tile nippers

Clean cloths

Protective gloves

Patio cleaner or dilute hydrochloric acid

Dust mask

Goggles

Notched trowel

Stiff, short-bristled stencil brush

Day One

Step 1

Cut bases from terra-cotta pots using a tile saw. Wear goggles and a dust mask to avoid breathing in fine particles, and work in a well-ventilated area.

Step 2

Experiment with your design on the cupboard front and lay out the design roughly on paper alongside the cupboard front.

Step 3

Scuff the surface of the cupboard front with a scuffing tool. Seal it with PVA adhesive diluted roughly 1 part PVA to 5 parts water.

Step 4

Spread adhesive evenly over the door recess. Embed the fork in the adhesive.

Step 5

Add pot bases and keys to build up a symmetrical pattern.

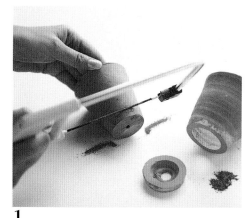

1

2

3

4

5

Cleaning mosaic thoroughly

Really bring out the sparkle in the keys and fork, and remove residual grout film, by cleaning the entire mosaic a few days after finishing it. Use patio cleaner or dilute hydrochloric acid. Wear protective gloves and goggles, and rinse the mosaic liberally with water afterwards. Polish with a clean, dry cloth.

8

6

7

Step 6

Wearing goggles, nip terra-cotta pot rims into small, narrow lengths and insert them into the adhesive to form a border. Use large sections to make smooth corners.

Step 7

Fill in the gaps with broken pot fragments, small pots, and pebbles. Nip smashed pot fragments into even smaller pieces, if necessary, using nippers. Build up the design more or less symmetrically, but allow the work to remain quite free, with the different sizes and shapes of fragments giving a spontaneous, fresh feel. Allow to set overnight.

Day Two

Step 8

Mix up powder grout using water in which PVA has been diluted in a ratio of approximately 1 part PVA to 5 parts water. Make the grout fairly stiff and dry. Wearing protective gloves, remove excess grout by scrubbing with a scouring pad and stiff, short-bristled stencil brush until all the mosaic elements are uncovered.

Découpage floral tiles

Découpage is updated in this fresh-as-a-daisy makeover for unattractive tiles. The motifs are simply cut from giftwrap.

Planning your time

DAY ONE
AM: Mask off and condition tiles; sponge on base color

PM: Sponge on second color; cut out floral motifs; glue in place; allow to dry overnight

DAY TWO
AM: Varnish

PM: Add subsequent coats of varnish, allowing each to dry before applying the next

Tools and materials

Giftwrap with floral motifs

Cold-set ceramic paints, matte varnish, and cleaner-conditioner (use same brand for compatibility)

Waterproof PVA adhesive

Masking tape

Palette

Protective gloves

Paintbrush and sponge

Paper towels (for cleaning tiles)

Craft knife and nail scissors

A frequently asked question is how to revamp unsightly tiles that would be expensive and very time-consuming to replace. Acres of horrible tiles evidently cover the globe!

This project was devised with this in mind and it incorporates both applied decoration in the form of découpage and a paint treatment that does not look homemade. Even viewed in unforgiving close-up, the tiles look as if they were purchased with this lively floral design on a vivid, painterly ground.

The key to producing a similarly convincing result is to be careful to match the painted background exactly to the giftwrap, so that the floral motif appears fully integrated with the ground color. Découpage was originally devised to mimic expensively hand-painted items, so you are continuing an age-old craft tradition by blending the cutout shape with the background in this way. Use good-quality giftwrap for a smooth finish.

The simple outlines of the flowers make the cutting out easy to do. If you are embarking on this project as an emergency makeover for really awful colored tiles, blank out the offending shade with tile primer and white tile paint before adding the sponged color and découpage motifs.

Day One

Step 1
Clean the tiles thoroughly.

Step 2
Using masking tape, mask off the tiles that are to remain plain.

Step 3
Apply tile conditioner to the tiles that are to be painted. Follow the manufacturer's directions precisely.

Step 4
Sponge the paler base color evenly over the tile, allowing some of the white tile to show through. Use only a tiny amount of paint on the sponge. The paint will dry almost immediately since the amount used is so minimal.

Step 5
Sponge the darker color on top of the lighter base. Allow to dry completely before applying floral motifs.

1

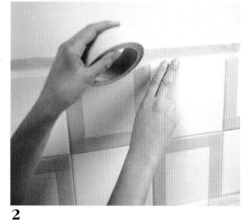

2

3

4

Choosing varnish

Matte varnish has been used here to provide a pleasing contrast with the shiny white tiles; but you may prefer a satin or a high-gloss finish, depending on the surface of the surrounding tiles. The more coats you apply, the more resilient the result.

5

8

6

7

Step 6
Cut motifs from giftwrap using nail scissors. Take care to remove all the background color from around the cutout motif.

Step 7
Using a solution of 1 part PVA adhesive and 1 part water, glue the flower motifs in the center of each sponged tile. Smooth out any air bubbles as the glue dries. If any large pockets of air form between parts of the paper and the tile, simply puncture these with a craft knife and they will flatten.

Day Two

Step 8
Remove the masking tape. Apply several coats of matte varnish, allowing each coat to dry thoroughly before applying the next.

White and silver crazy mosaic pots

Inexpensive machine-made terra-cotta pots attain designer status with a sprinkling of silver tesserae and a coating of smart white tiles, adding a touch of glamour to your planting.

Container gardening is always popular. Plants can be moved around to suit the seasons and to give an ever-changing display both in and out of the house. However, one problem with growing plants in containers is that the plants keep growing! It sometimes seems that no sooner has a plant been repotted than it grows enthusiastically out of its new container. Keeping up can become quite expensive, particularly since some plants achieve substantial sizes. Machine-made terra-cotta pots are an affordable solution but they are are not always inspiring to look at.

The simplest ideas are often the most effective. Here, inexpensive reject tiles in classic white have been smashed into random fragments and applied to pots interspersed with bands of sparkling, silvery-mirrored tesserae. Using waterproof tile adhesive and grout, and carefully sealing the porous surface of the pot before starting to mosaic, they are as robust as they are striking.

Suitable for sunroom or garden applications, these pots can be left outside even in cold weather. If you live in a cold climate, make sure you use frostproof grout. When the fall marigolds have faded, they can be replaced with evergreen topiary spheres whose architectural shape will complement the pots.

A few days after completion, when the grout has hardened, you may want to give the mosaic an additional cleaning with hydrochloric acid or patio cleaner. This gives the finished pots an unbeatable sparkle. Wear goggles and protective gloves and work in a well-ventilated area. After cleaning, rinse the pots liberally with water before drying with a soft cloth.

Planning your time

DAY ONE
AM: Seal pots; plan border size; smash and apply white tiles to interior and exterior; cut white tiles into lengths, then squares, to cover rim

PM: Apply white tiles to rim; apply mirrored tesserae to border or spiral

DAY TWO
AM: Grout

Tools and materials

Terra-cotta pots

White tiles

Waterproof PVA adhesive

Masking tape

Paintbrush

Mid-gray frostproof powder grout

Pencil or chalk

Burlap

Wooden tongue depressors

Goggles

Protective gloves

Hammer

Tile cutter

Tile nippers

Mirrored tesserae

Patio cleaner or dilute hydrochloric acid

Clean cloths

Day One

Step 1

If the pots are for exterior use, and are not frostproof, seal inside and out by brushing on a solution of 1 part waterproof PVA adhesive and 1 part water.

Step 2

Place a few mirrored tesserae on the pot to assess the width of the band or spiral you require. Remember to allow enough space for grout between the tesserae and between the edge of the band and the rest of the mosaic. Using masking tape, draw the position of the design roughly with pencil or chalk.

Step 3

Wearing goggles and protective gloves, break up the white tiles using a hammer. Wrap them individually in burlap and tap sharply at the center. Open the burlap to check that the tile is sufficiently broken. Close the burlap and repeat until pieces are the desired size.

Step 4

Apply tiles around the border of the pot, using waterproof PVA. For a professional look, place the glazed, rounded-off edge of the tile next to the border.

Step 5

Wearing goggles and gloves, use nippers to break tiles further if necessary to fit. Hold the nippers with the curved side against the tile, just in from the edge and snip cleanly. Glue on pieces of white tile to cover all parts of the pot except for what will be the mirrored band and the top of the rim. Continue the white tiles down inside the pot to approximately the point that will become the soil fill-level. This gives a solid look to the finished pot. Keep the cracks between the pieces even.

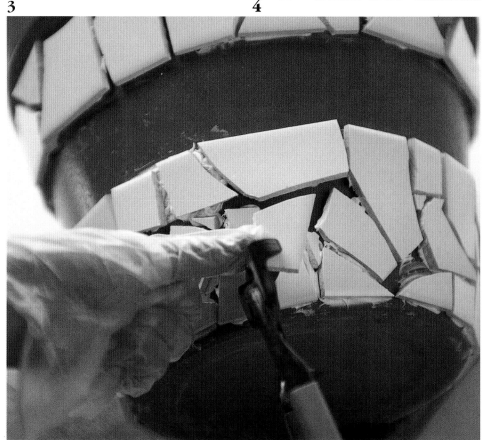

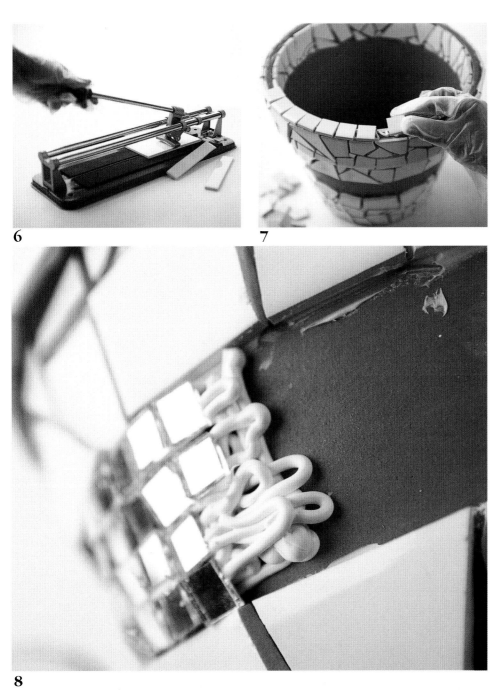

6

7

8

Step 6
Cut lengths of white tile on a tile cutter, to a width that will sit neatly across the top of the pot rim, spanning the thickness of the rim and the tiles already applied to the interior and exterior of the pot.

Step 7
Nip the long strips into smaller pieces, roughly square, and glue on with waterproof PVA to cover the rim of the pot. Do not worry about calculating the circumference and dividing it equally by the number of tiles. Simply adjust the gap between each tile minutely as you complete the rim mosaic. The eye will absorb any tiny adjustment and read the rim tiles as being evenly spaced.

Step 8
Since the mirrored tesserae are much thinner than the white tiles, you will need to build up quite a thick layer of waterproof PVA before applying the defining spiral or bands of mirrored tile in order to keep them level with the surface of the white tiles. When you have finished, allow to set overnight.

Day Two

Step 9
Mix frostproof gray grout with water that has had waterproof PVA added in a ratio of approximately 1 part PVA to 5 parts water. Aim for a dryish, mud-pie consistency. Wearing gloves and using a wooden tongue depressor, apply the grout to the mosaic, taking care to push it well into all the cracks. Rub away excess grout with a dry cloth.

9

Making mosaic tiles

As well as being the most affordable option, machine-made tiles are the ideal choice for mosaic projects; they are thinner than their more expensive, handmade counterparts and therefore smash and nip easily. Most tile suppliers have a selection of seconds, or visit a factory store for affordable inspiration.

China patchwork doorstep

A neglected, age-worn doorstep becomes a real show stopper bedecked in irresistibly pretty broken china. Patterned saucers add interest and color to the front of the step.

The doorstep is generally ignored as an opportunity for applied decoration. However, since it is one of the first details visitors see as they approach your home, it is worth spending a little effort to make it into a real focal point that will lift the spirits.

Many of us are inveterate purchasers and hoarders of mismatched china—particularly pretty saucers, which are usually inexpensive at garage sales, junk shops, and flea markets. However, there is a limit to the number of plates and saucers that you can hang on the walls without making your home look like an "olde worlde tea shoppe." This project justifies your china shopping expeditions admirably.

Small saucers decorate the vertical front of the step, sized to suit the step. An old toy tea set would yield adorable tiny china plates and saucers for a shallow step. The gaps between the saucers are filled with broken china fragments, predominantly in white in order to focus attention on the saucers themselves. The gaps could also be filled with broken tiles.

On the horizontal surface of the step, the saucer motif is picked up by replicating their round shapes in mosaic, using sections of flat plate rims to define each round shape while producing a long-wearing, practical flat surface. Again, the gaps are filled with china and tile fragments.

Planning your time

DAY ONE
AM: Scuff step; "fit" and attach saucers to front of step; apply bed of adhesive; allow to dry

PM: Smash/nip china and apply to fill in gaps between saucers; apply roundels to top of step; allow to set overnight

DAY TWO
AM: Grout

Tools and materials

Saucers

Plates with pretty rims

Plates with pretty centers

White china

Patio cleaner or dilute hydrochloric acid

Scrap china or discarded tesserae

Tile nippers

Protective gloves

Goggles

Scuffing tool (nails driven through piece of scrap wood)

Waterproof PVA adhesive

Chalk

Scouring pads

Clean cloths

Stiff, short-bristled stencil brush

Hammer and burlap

Wooden tongue depressors

Gray waterproof tile adhesive

Gray frostproof powder grout

Day One

Step 1

Scuff the surface of the step and seal with PVA adhesive that is diluted approximately 1 part PVA to 5 parts water.

Step 2

Trial fit the saucers to the front surface of the step. Mark out their positions with chalk.

Step 3

Liberally spread tile adhesive on the bottom of each saucer and to the front of the step just inside the circled area that marks the saucer position. Apply the saucer to the front of the step.

Step 4

Fill in the area around the saucers with a thick bed of adhesive, making sure that it completely fills the area beneath the sloped underside of each saucer. Build up the depth of adhesive until it is almost level with the saucer rims. You are aiming to produce the impression that the saucers are embedded within a solid step rather than having been applied to the surface, as well as to provide a strong, solid surface that will withstand pedestrian traffic. Allow to dry.

Step 5

Wearing gloves and goggles, wrap the china in folded burlap and smash it into pieces with a hammer. Then nip predominantly white china into smaller, triangular pieces. Smash and nip colored and patterned plate rims to make circular motifs on top of the step.

1

2

3

4

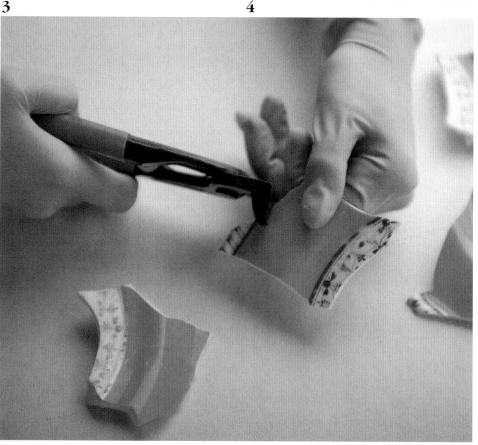

5

6

7

8

9

10

Step 6

Apply white triangular fragments to fill the gaps on the front of the step. Prop up lower triangles if necessary with scraps of china or discarded tesserae.

Step 7

"Butter" individual fragments and apply them to build up a roundel design on the horizontal surface of the step. Be very careful to embed the china evenly. Since the china is probably of varying thickness, you will need to push thick pieces well down into the adhesive, and build up adhesive thickly behind thinner pieces to bring them up to the same level. Try to produce as flat a surface as possible.

Step 8

Fill in areas around the roundels with white fragments. Allow to dry overnight.

Day Two

Step 9

Mix PVA adhesive into water in a ratio of approximately 1 part PVA to 5 parts water. Use this water to mix the grout to a dryish, mud-pie consistency. Wearing protective gloves, spread the grout liberally over the mosaic, working in one area at a time.

Step 10

Push the grout well into the gaps. Remove the excess as you work with a dry cloth and scouring pads. Remove tricky bits of grout with a stiff-bristled stencil brush. Give the mosaic a final cleaning a couple of days after completing, with patio cleaner or dilute hydrochloric acid, to bring out the full sparkle of the mosaic. Wear goggles and gloves during handling. Rinse the step thoroughly afterwards with clean water; then, polish with a soft cloth.

Playing card mosaic backsplash

This intricate-looking mosaic effect, created from just a few playing cards, gives new life to old tiles. This project opens endless possibilities since so many designs are available.

Playing cards are ideally suited to many applications where tiles are commonly used. They are already sealed with a durable plastic finish, and their crisp, geometric designs lend themselves readily to reproducing seemingly complex mosaic effects at minimal cost and effort.

The cobalt blue color scheme used here is a perennial winner for bathrooms, and it is easy to find playing cards like these in stationery and toy stores.

Junk shops also can yield an interesting selection of inexpensive old playing cards with richly textural

designs on the reverse. Many of these sets of cards are incomplete and of no use to card players. Even if the cards have been much handled, by peeling away the layers of the playing card to leave only the patterned, uppermost layer, you are left with a thin, strong, coated paper that is perfectly clean and usefully slightly raised on the side that needs to stick to the tile. This laborious, but critical, step also means that fewer layers of varnish need to be added once the mosaic is assembled in order to achieve a flat, long-wearing surface. The more layers of varnish you add, the more professional it will look.

If the intricate placing of the tiny components seems like an unbearably fussy task, simply apply the patterns more or less whole, without breaking them down into smaller parts. The effect may not have quite such a mosaic-type look, but will still be very striking.

Planning your time
....

DAY ONE
AM: Clean tiles; experiment with design; peel off card fronts; cut card fronts into smaller units; apply outer border

PM: Mark out grid; apply internal border and squares; apply tiny squares at the intersection of each inner border

DAY TWO
AM: Paint diluted PVA over tiles; allow to dry; varnish and let dry

PM: Apply additional coats of varnish

Tools and materials
....

Pack of playing cards

Waterproof PVA adhesive

Glass cleaner and paper towels

Craft knife

Small paintbrush

Acrylic varnish

Pencil

Ruler

Graph paper

Small scissors

Cotton swabs

Wooden skewers

Overhead projector marker pen

Day One

Step 1
Clean the tiles thoroughly with glass cleaner to remove any hint of grease.

Step 2
Cut up some card reverses into smaller units and borders. Experiment with your design. Calculate and roughly draw out how many smaller units are necessary to produce the nine blocks in this design, depending on the size of the tiles you are decorating.

Step 3
Peel the reverse of the playing cards away from the fronts so that you are left with one thin layer of coated paper.

Step 4
Cut the thinned card reverse into smaller components as needed for your design—for example, blocks of four-flower motifs, single motifs, and lengths of borders.

Step 5
Mix a solution of 1 part waterproof PVA adhesive and 1 part water. Glue the outer borders. Be careful not to glue layers of paper on top of each other at the corners; it will produce too much bulk. Instead, overlap the layers, then trim the intersection neatly and cleanly with a craft knife.

Making it last

Although durable and washable, this project, like all those involving applied layers, is not ideally suited to applications where it would have to withstand a constant onslaught of water, such as shower walls.

1

2

3

4

5

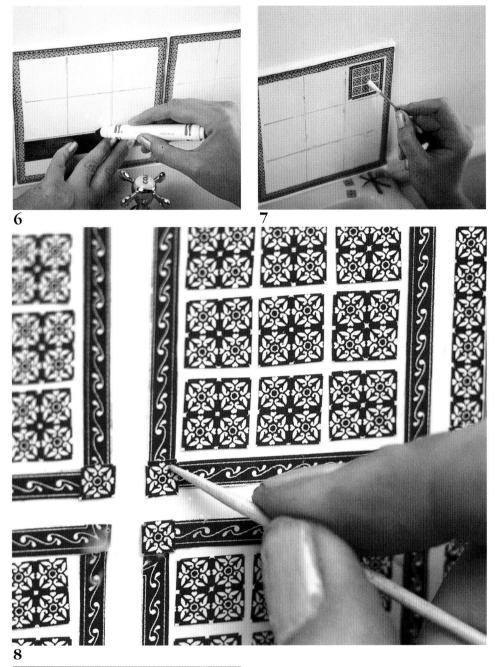

6

7

8

9

Step 6
Using an overhead projector marker pen, divide the tile into a grid forming nine squares.

Step 7
Spread dilute PVA adhesive over one of the smaller squares formed by the grid. Apply a narrow border in a square within this. Fill this square with small blocks, evenly spaced. Make any adjustments of position by using a cotton swab to ease the small component parts of the design gently into place.

Step 8
Finish off each corner of the newly formed square border with a single block. With a craft knife, cut away excess layers of paper beneath the block to minimize paper bulk. Adjust the position using a wooden skewer, since the pieces are very small and hard to handle. Build up the remaining eight blocks in the same way. Do not worry if the gaps between pieces are not identical.

Day Two

Step 9
Apply one coat of diluted PVA to the tile, then several coats of varnish. Allow the manufacturer's recommended drying time between coats.

Sorting the tesserae

For ease in working, sort the tiny card tesserae into envelopes according to their individual sizes. Cut the pieces out over the weekend and in the evening prior to making the project to save time.

Gilded window recess

This evocative "gilded" tile treatment is both pretty and practical, and very easy to achieve. It is best reserved for areas not in constant contact with water.

Window recesses offer the perfect opportunity to indulge in dramatic decorating effects that might be overwhelming if used more liberally. Since this is an area usually overlooked by even the most fervent decorator, making your window recess more of a central feature of the room is guaranteed to induce gasps of admiration from all who see it. Even more satisfying is watching people's faces as you reveal the humble beginnings of this beautiful design. They will never believe that such a rich, multilayered effect started life as plain, reject tiles.

Lettering in all its forms is very versatile as a decorative motif. You can, of course, use old deeds and letters if you are lucky enough to have some, and photocopy them to achieve similar effects, but in order to make this project truly achievable in a weekend we have supplied a page of copperplate Latin script and devised an alphabet on page 76 ready for photocopying.

Metal leaf is now widely available in craft stores and by mail order, and gilding of this random nature is satisfyingly simple. Children enjoy flicking the coffee granules onto the tiles and do so in a more relaxed, sporadic way than adults ever will. If you cannot borrow a small child, loosen up as best you can and enjoy the thrill of legitimately flinging coffee at the walls! Like most decorative effects, the result looks dreadful while in the process, but it is suddenly wonderful on completion.

Planning your time

DAY ONE
AM: Plan tiling; cut tiles to fit; tile recess and allow to set

PM: Photocopy alphabet and script; cut out blocks of text to cover tiles; cut out individual words and letters

DAY TWO
AM: Grout tiles and clean

PM: Apply text to each tile; age with coffee and tea; apply metal leaf, words, and letters; varnish

Tools and materials

Gold-colored metal leaf

Acrylic gold size

Paintbrush

Scissors and/or a craft knife and cutting mat (optional)

Freeze-dried coffee granules

Three tea bags

Shellac or acrylic varnish

Tiles, any color

Templates on page 76

Buff-colored powder grout

Universal stains in ocher and burnt umber

Clean cloths and paper towels

PVA adhesive

Scuffing tool (nails driven through piece of scrap wood)

Tile adhesive

Notched trowel

Tile spacers

Glass cleaner

Protective gloves

Tile squeegee

Tracing paper and soft pencil

Masking tape

Plastic bag and rolling pin

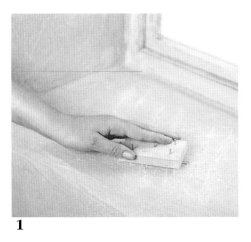

1

Day One

Step 1

Scuff the surface of the window recess with the scuffing tool to provide a key, or rough surface, for the tile adhesive. Seal with a solution of 1 part PVA adhesive and 1 part water.

Step 2

Roughly try out the tile spacing to ascertain whether any cuts are necessary to fit them properly. On the horizontal surface, place tiles from the center of the sill outward. Spread tile adhesive onto the horizontal surface of the recess. Use the notched trowel to achieve a uniform thickness of adhesive. Apply the tiles.

Step 3

Apply the tiles to the vertical surfaces of the recess. Start at the bottom and work upward, making any cuts necessary at the top of the recess. Use tile spacers between each one to keep them evenly spaced as the adhesive sets.

2

3

4

5

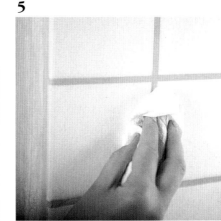

6

7

8

Step 4

Mark out the size of the tile onto tracing paper. Photocopy the Templates on page 76 to the required sizes. Place the tracing of the tile size over a sheet of text to ascertain a pleasing placement of the lettering within the tile. Transfer the corner marks onto the sheet of text and cut out with scissors or a craft knife. Repeat until you have sufficient pre-cut sheets to cover all the tiles.

Step 5

Cut individual letters from the alphabet and enlarged words from script photocopies using scissors and/or a craft knife.

Day Two

Step 6

Mix PVA adhesive with water, approximately 1 part PVA to 5 parts water, and color this mixture with ocher and burnt umber universal stains. Use this water to make up the powder grout to a dryish, mud-pie consistency. Apply with a tile squeegee and remove excess with a dry cloth or paper towel.

Step 7

Thoroughly clean the tiles using glass cleaner and paper towels for a lint-free result.

Step 8

Mix a solution of 1 part PVA adhesive and 1 part water, apply it to the tiles, and affix the sheets of script. Run text alternately vertically and horizontally to achieve a richly textured, random look.

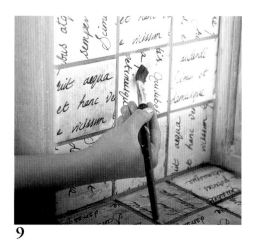

9

Step 9

Make a strong cup of tea (three tea bags in a mug produces a good dyeing brew). Allow to cool before brushing all over the script-covered tiles. Let it drip onto the grout for an aged effect. Add more tea randomly and allow to pool to form an attractive antiqued look.

Step 10

Roughly grind freeze-dried instant coffee granules in a mortar and pestle or in a plastic bag with a rolling pin, until some forms powder and some forms slightly smaller granules. Mask off surrounding areas and fling coffee over the tiles for an age-spotted effect.

Step 11

Apply acrylic gold size randomly to the tiles using a small paintbrush. Leave for approximately 15 minutes or until clear and tacky, rather than opaque and wet.

10

Using different colors

This project would look very different using silver-colored leaf (aluminum). Photocopy the text in black and white to produce a dark gray color, and instead of tea dyeing, color the script with dilute blue ink. Exchange the coffee spattering for ink spattered from an old toothbrush. Mask off the surrounding area!

11

12

13

14

Step 12

Press a sheet of metal (gold-colored) leaf against each tile using a gentle pressing motion through a paper towel in order not to tear the fragile metal. Allow to set for a few minutes before brushing away excess with a dry paintbrush. Burnish with a soft cloth.

Step 13

Using the dilute PVA solution, apply letters and words randomly across all the tiles. A particularly attractive, handmade look occurs where words and letters flow across two or more tiles. Cut out that part of the letter that would cross in the grout line and discard.

Step 14

Varnish the tiles with several coats of shellac for a pleasing rich, golden tone, allowing each coat to dry thoroughly before applying the next. Try to keep the varnish away from the grout; the contrast of the matte grout and the smooth sheen of the tiles is particularly appealing. For a faster result, simply brush over the entire surface.

Mosaic mirror frame

A modern classic in a restrained coffee and caramel palette, this simple-to-make frame includes mirrored tesserae and provides the perfect project for the novice mosaicist.

When you visit a supplier of mosaic tiles, allow plenty of time. It is guaranteed that you will become overwhelmed by the array of color and texture that greets you. Even the more experienced can still be rather bewildered when confronted with what seems at first like a never-ending number of choices in color and texture.

When you have settled down you will realize that most suppliers have duplicate tesserae in various formats. Loose tiles are often available, sometimes sold in bargain mixed bags, although you will then have to make do with the colors supplied, which may tend to be rather bright and not at all in keeping with the sophisticated feel intended for this project. Tiles are also sold in sheets of varying sizes, and by weight. The store's staff will be able to advise you on the most economical way to buy for the size of project you are planning.

This mirror frame is a satisfyingly fast-growing project, and can be made using just a few small sheets of glass tesserae and a bag of mirrored tesserae. Although you can change the colors to suit your own decorating scheme, it is recommended that you stick to a limited palette for the most professional, elegant results. Aim for a mirror that looks as if it has emerged from a chic designer store rather than from a flea market.

Planning your time

DAY ONE
AM: Mask off mirror; scuff and seal frame; cut tesserae into quarters and roughly plan design; cut mirrored tesserae to fit inner and outer edges of the frame

PM: Apply adhesive and tiles to edges and flat face of frame

DAY TWO
AM: Grout

Tools and materials

Mirror in flat profile frame

Masking tape

Mirrored square tesserae

Glass tesserae in caramel, copper, black, and coffee shades

Scuffing tool (nails driven through piece of scrap wood)

PVA adhesive

Paintbrush

Tile nippers

Goggles and protective gloves

Wooden skewers

Wooden tongue depressors

Tile adhesive

White powder grout

Clean cloths

Scouring pads

Stiff, short-bristled stencil brush

Patio cleaner or dilute hydrochloric acid

1

Day One

Step 1
Mask off the mirror with masking tape.

Step 2
Scuff the frame with a scuffing tool to provide a good key, or rough surface, for the adhesive.

Step 3
Seal the frame with a solution of 1 part PVA adhesive and 1 part water. This provides an even better key for good adhesion and seals the frame against dampness, which could cause the mosaic to lift off.

2

3

Finding a frame

Most mosaic suppliers have a range of flat frames that are perfect for this project. Alternately, use this method to jazz up a junk-shop find or a chain-store bargain.

4

5

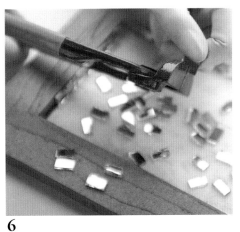

6

Step 4

Wearing goggles and gloves, cut the glass tesserae into halves, then into quarters with nippers. Place the curved side of the nippers toward the tile, just a tiny way across the tile. Exert equal pressure on the opposite side of the tile with your thumb and forefinger as you press the nippers together. The tile should break neatly in half, but do not worry if it does not; tesserae do not always break as expected, even for the most skilled mosaicist.

Step 5

Experiment laying out the tesserae on the frame to ascertain whether more cuts are necessary, and to gauge the spacing between tiles.

Step 6

Cut the mirrored tesserae to fit in the area between the surface of the mirror and the flat face of the frame.

7

Step 7

Glue the cut mirrored tesserae to the inner edge of the frame with tile adhesive. Make sure you leave even gaps between tesserae.

Step 8

Cut, if cuts are necessary, more mirrored tesserae to place around the outer edge of the frame. Apply these to the outer edge.

Step 9

Apply mirrored and colored tesserae onto the flat face of the frame in a random checkerboard pattern. In this direct method of mosaic the tesserae are applied with the ridged side down. The tiles should sit butted up against the tiles covering the inner and outer edges of the frame, but leaving enough room for grout beneath. The mirrored tiles are much thinner than the colored glass tiles, so allow them to sit on the surface of the adhesive, but push the thicker tiles well down into it. This will give a smooth, flat surface. Take care to leave sufficient space for grout by removing any adhesive that creeps up around the tesserae. A wooden skewer is perfect for this fussy but necessary task. Allow to dry overnight.

8

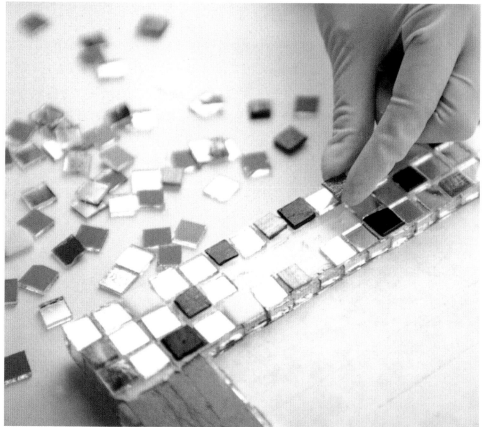

9

10

11

Day Two

Step 10

Mix up the grout using water that has PVA added in a ratio of approximately 1 part PVA to 5 parts water for greater adhesion to the frame. Make the grout fairly stiff and dry. Grout vertical, then horizontal surfaces, using a tongue depressor as a spreader. Work in all directions, pressing the grout well into all the gaps.

Step 11

Wearing gloves to protect your hands from any sharp, protruding tesserae, rub off excess grout with a dry cloth. Remove any remaining grout with an abrasive pad and/or a stiff-bristled stencil brush. Give the mosaic a final cleaning a few days after completion using patio cleaner or dilute hydrochloric acid. Wear goggles and gloves, and wash off well with copious amounts of water before polishing with a soft cloth.

Making mirrored tesserae

Mirrored tesserae, although convenient, are comparatively expensive. You could make your own tesserae by cutting down a mirror tile with a glass cutter. Wear goggles and gloves to protect your eyes and hands from flying shards of glass.

Memorabilia china fountain

This whimsical fountain gives a new lease on life to broken china that you just cannot bear to throw away. It makes a stunning garden feature, with its perpetually pouring teapot.

Everyone has experienced the heart-sinking moment when a favorite piece of china jumps from your slippery hand onto the hard floor, emerging rather less intact than is useful. It feels almost unbearably brutal simply to discard the cherished item, particularly when the piece is largely complete except for a hairline crack or chipped rim.

If you have been hoarding broken china for years, never knowing quite what to do with those treasured fragments of your family's history— your daughter's first plate, wedding china, a childhood cereal bowl—this charming fountain recycles them all to produce a uniquely personal fountain.

Children of all ages will enjoy picking out their favorite pieces from long ago, with the added appeal of the china being featured in a simple fountain. No one will guess that such a richly decorative fountain started life as a cheap plastic wall planter and a sheet of wood, which makes the project doubly satisfying. You could also mosaic over an existing fountain.

An inexpensive self-contained pump, the pipe fed through the spout of a beloved broken teapot, provides the water flow. A simple backing board of exterior-grade plywood is a sturdy weatherproof support, and the planter forms the splash pool. The diverse elements are unified by sticking to a limited color range of rose pink, white, and cobalt blue highlighted with gold. Planted tea cups add a contrast in texture and the planting can be changed seasonally. Drill holes in the cup bases if more drainage is needed. If you live in a cold climate make sure you use frostproof tile adhesive.

A final cleaning with patio cleaner or dilute hydrochloric acid will make your mosaic fountain sparkle. Be sure to rinse off well.

Planning your time

DAY ONE
AM: Mark and cut out plywood shape; screw bowl onto wood; mark out key elements; drill pipe holes; feed through water pipe and cable; glue teapot and pipe

PM: Make mosaic

DAY TWO
AM: Grout

Tools and materials

¾" (19mm) exterior-grade plywood and 1x2" (25x50mm) softwood

Tape measure, tracing paper, pencil, masking tape, and chalk

Scouring pads, short-bristled stencil brush, and clean cloths

Jigsaw or coping saw

Flat-backed plastic planter

Screws, D ring, and screwdriver

Pump

Drill and ¾" (19mm) flat drill bit

3' (1m) plastic pipe, diameter to match pump outlet size

8" (20cm) of 1½" (38mm) plastic waste pipe

Waterproof epoxy adhesive

Gray waterproof tile adhesive

Waterproof PVA adhesive

Gray frostproof powder grout

Broken china (including cups, teapot, and saucers), beads, and buttons

Varnish and paintbrush

Tile nippers, hammer, and burlap

Goggles and protective gloves

Scuffing tool (nails driven through piece of scrap wood)

Patio cleaner or dilute hydrochloric acid

Day One

Step 1

Mark out half of the scroll-topped shape that forms the backboard of the fountain onto tracing paper. Mark a central line down the length of the plywood piece, then trace the design onto one half of the plywood. Turn the tracing paper over and trace the same lines onto the other half to ensure a symmetrical design. Cut along the lines with an electric jigsaw or a coping saw.

Step 2

Screw a flat-backed plastic planter onto the plywood shape at the base to form the splash bowl.

Step 3

Scuff the surface of the wood using a scuffing tool to provide a good key, or rough surface, for the tile adhesive.

Step 4

Seal the wood backboard and bowl with a solution of 1 part waterproof PVA and 1 part water.

Step 5

Roughly lay out the key elements of the design; for example, the teapot, plates, saucers, etc. Chalk out the position of these elements on the board.

1

2

3

4

5

Assembling pieces of china

This project is quite labor intensive and involves vast quantities of china nibbled into tiny pieces to produce a really rich, textural result. As such, you may want to begin assembling your "pool" of nibbled pieces during the evenings of the week prior to making the fountain. Mosaic is undoubtedly more relaxing when you have lots of pre-cut, pre-sorted pieces to choose from as you work.

6

Step 6

Using a ¾" (19mm) flat drill bit, drill a hole behind the teapot position to take the water pipe. Drill a second hole through the wood and bowl, above the water line in one corner. This will take the water pipe and the electric cable.

Step 7

Place the pump in the splash bowl. Feed the water pipe leading from the pump through the lower hole in the backboard from front to back; then up and through the upper hole, from back to front. The water pipe is now placed to feed into the teapot and through the spout.

Step 8

Attach a short length of wide pipe to the pool internally to cover the second drilled hole. Use waterproof epoxy adhesive, securing with masking tape until the glue has set. This wider pipe allows you to feed the water pipe unobtrusively up and around the back of the board to allow the water to recirculate. The electric cable from the pump can also be fed through this pipe to conceal it. The wide pipe will be covered in mosaic to blend in with the rest of the fountain. The water pipe and electric cable can be fed back through this channel to remove the pump for annual cleaning and servicing.

7

8

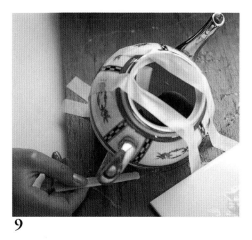

9

Step 9

Spread epoxy adhesive around the teapot area. Attach the teapot, angling the spout down and out toward the bowl of the fountain. Hold it with masking tape until the glue has set.

Step 10

Attach other key elements of the design, such as pot lids and teacup halves, using a thick bed of waterproof, gray tile adhesive.

Step 11

Break up the remaining china into manageable fragments. Do this by using first a hammer, tapped against the china wrapped in burlap, then nippers. Wear gloves and goggles as protection.

Grinding the teapot spout

If your teapot has not broken at an obliging angle, you can cut it to fit by using an angle grinder, available from tool rental stores. Wear protective ear muffs, goggles, and gloves when using it. An angle grinder will also cut cups neatly in half. It is possible to nip and sand china to size without recourse to this power tool, but performing this task by hand is infinitely slower and results in a greater number of undesirable breakages.

10

11

14

12

Step 12

Build up the mosaic by working a small area at a time. Work symmetrically to achieve good visual balance; for example, if applying blue china to one side of the scroll top, build up the other side simultaneously. Cover the entire fountain in mosaic, using beads, buttons—anything that is pretty and has significance for you. Protect any vulnerable items with varnish.

Day Two

Step 13

Mix frostproof gray powder grout with water to which waterproof PVA has been added in a ratio of 1 part PVA to 5 parts water. Aim for a dryish, mud-pie consistency. Wearing gloves, work the grout well into every crack and crevice of the design. Remove excess with dry cloths, scouring pads, and a stiff stencil brush.

Step 14

Screw a small piece of 1x2" (25x50mm) softwood to the back of the fountain at the top; screw a D ring (available from hardware stores) onto this. Fix a second piece of 1x2" (25x50mm) softwood to the bottom of the panel, behind the splash pool; this will provide a spacer so that the water pipe that runs up behind the fountain does not get crushed.

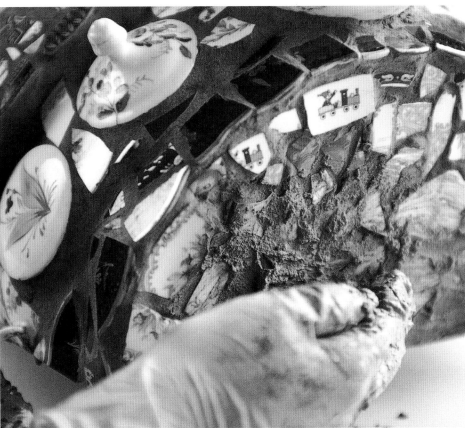

13

Daisy mosaic table

This design of daisies created from broken, reject tiles transforms a dilapidated junk-shop table into an attractive and useful piece of garden furniture.

T his table base with its faded green paint was found languishing outside a junk shop. The top had completely disintegrated long ago and the base itself was somewhat unstable, but the delicate proportions and gentle color were perfect. Even the rust spots were evocative of summers past.

Hammered into shape, the wobbly nature of the base improved considerably, but it was necessary to have a new top cut from exterior-grade plywood. Small, independent lumber yards are usually happy to supply a custom cutting service for a small price. If you are mosaicing an existing tabletop, scuff and seal first of all.

The very cheapest, machine-made tiles are perfect for mosaic because they are thin and you can cut them with blissful ease. Those used here are seconds from a factory outlet. The pieces are relatively large in order to give the design a strong, graphic look, so the work progresses with satisfying speed. Be sure with all mosaic work to consider the grout lines as elements that are as important as the mosaic pieces themselves. Leave gaps of equal width so that there is a pleasing flow between pieces to produce a cohesive end result rather than the effect of an ill-fitting jigsaw. Remember, when choosing your tiles, that the green color for the stems needs to be of a dramatically darker tone than that used in the background, or the trailing stem and leaf design will simply be lost in the ground color. The background was produced from a mixture of toning shades for a softly textured look, but you could stick to just one color for a more striking contrast. If you live in a cold climate and the table is going to be left outdoors, make sure you use frostproof grout and adhesive.

Planning your time

DAY ONE
AM: Scuff and seal tabletop; mark out design; prepare pieces of tile for daisies, leaves, stems, and table edge; apply flower motifs, leaves, and stem

PM: Smash and cut tiles for background; apply background and edging tiles

DAY TWO
AM: Grout

Tools and materials

Table base and top

New tabletop (if necessary) cut from exterior-grade plywood

Waterproof PVA adhesive

Scuffing tool (nails driven through piece of scrap wood)

Hammer and burlap

Paintbrush

Chalk

Clean cloths

Tiles (ivory, yellow, dark green, beige, aqua, and pale green)

Tile nippers

Tile cutter

Sanding block

Gray frostproof powder grout

Gray frostproof, waterproof tile adhesive—for example, swimming-pool tile adhesive

Wooden tongue depressors

Goggles

Protective gloves

Patio cleaner or dilute hydrochloric acid

Scouring pads

Stiff, short-bristled stencil brush

Day One

Step 1
Scuff the surface of the table using a scuffing tool.

Step 2
Brush on a solution of 1 part waterproof PVA adhesive and 1 part water to seal the wood against moisture. Allow to dry.

Step 3
Draw on the design very roughly using chalk. All you need are circles to represent the positions of the daisies and single lines to represent the stems. Follow the Templates on page 77 to help you with the design.

Step 4
Wearing goggles and gloves, place the ivory, dark green, and yellow tiles individually between layers of burlap, then smash each one in the center with a hammer. Open the burlap to see how the tile has broken. If necessary, fold the burlap back over the tile and hit with the hammer again until you have several large triangular pieces.

Step 5
Still wearing goggles and gloves, use tile nippers to shape the shards of yellow tile into approximate circles for the daisy centers. Nip some in half to form semicircles, so that some daisies span the edge of the table. This gives a fresh, spontaneous feel to the design, as if the daisy chain is truly scattered across the surface of the table.

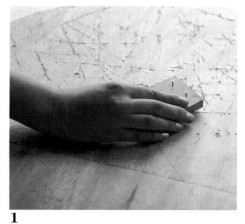

1

2

3

4

5

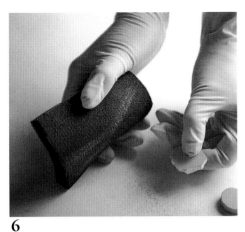

6

Step 6

Sand the daisy centers with a sanding block to remove jagged edges, but allow them to remain imperfectly round. Calculated imperfection is a distinctive element of the finished design; perfect circles would look awkward with the graphic petals.

Step 7

Some of the larger triangular pieces of dark green and ivory tile may need slight nipping to produce appropriately sized pieces to represent the petals and leaf shapes. Again, do not try to produce realistic petal shapes. Keep the shapes starkly angular.

Step 8

"Butter" each tessera on the reverse with tile adhesive, using a wooden tongue depressor. Then apply the flower centers and petals to the table, loosely following the chalk marks. Do not try to keep strictly within the chalked circles or the design will look too forced. Aim for a feeling of spontaneity, using the tile pieces almost as you break them rather than worrying about finding the perfectly shaped petal.

7

8

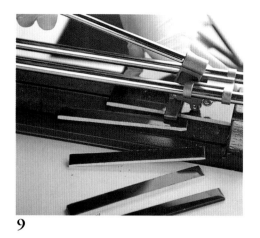

9

Step 9

Cut strips of dark green tile on the tile cutter to form the stems. The required width will depend on the scale of your design. These strips are approximately ¾" (1.5cm) wide, making a good visual balance to the flower heads, which are around 8" (20cm) across. From the four outside edges of a tile only, cut strips from your chosen background color the thickness of the tabletop, plus one tile thickness—these will be used for the mosaic band placed around the edge of the table.

Step 10

Nip the resulting long strips into smaller pieces. The edging pieces look neatest when cut into squares, while the stems look best when cut into random lengths.

Step 11

"Butter" and apply the stems and leaves as you applied the flowers.

10

11

12

13

14

15

Step 12

Create a "pool" of randomly mixed background color by smashing, then nipping, beige, pale green, and aqua tiles into pieces approximately ¾" (1.5cm) square. Do not aim for perfect regularity in the shapes produced.

Step 13

"Butter" and apply the background pieces, taking care to preserve even grout spacing.

Step 14

"Butter" and apply the edge pieces, taking care to line up the glazed edge of the tile with the surface of the table for a smooth finish.

Day Two

Step 15

Mix up the powder grout, incorporating waterproof PVA adhesive in a ratio of approximately 1 part PVA to 5 parts water before you mix. This gives the grout increased adhesion to the wooden tabletop. Mix the grout to a dryish, mud-pie consistency and press well into the gaps between the tiles. Because the tiles are not necessarily of uniform thickness, you may find it easier to grout with your fingers (protected by gloves) rather than a squeegee. Rub away any excess grout with a clean, dry cloth and scouring pads. A stiff, short-bristled stencil brush is also useful for removing grout from the corners of mosaic pieces. A few days after completion, clean the mosaic with patio cleaner or dilute hydrochloric acid. Wear goggles and gloves and wash off the solution with plenty of water.

Safety advice

Remember that the edges of glazed smashed or nipped tiles are essentially broken glass. Wear gloves when working with broken tiles and handle all the pieces carefully.

"Antique" tiled fireplace

Here, tiles painted in an "antique" style decorate a fireplace. The classic-looking top could also be applied to an area above a shelf or cupboard for a formal look.

Who can resist buying tiles from factory outlets and flea markets! However, you usually find that they sit around being used as makeshift pot stands and trivets while awaiting a project more worthy of their beauty. These charming Delft-style tiles were a case in point.

In this project, plain tiles and inexpensive rejects give a striking change of scale and stretch a meager initial supply of Delft tiles. Hand painted with ceramic paints to mimic old tiles, they integrate perfectly with the pretty floral motifs. You may get lucky and find large hand-painted tiles in a junk shop, but it is much more satisfying to paint your own. Also, you can be sure of having two end tiles of exactly the same size, and at a considerably reduced cost than their antiquated equivalent.

Although the tiles in this project have been used to dress up a fireplace, you could also run a decorative border of tiles around a room, or highlight a small area of a room, such as a window or door, by adding a mix-and-match border of junk shop and reject tiles and your own hand-painted ones.

The formal pediment, which gives such a smart, classical look, is simply assembled from cheap home-improvement store moldings and two plate shelves. Do not be put off by the technical-looking miter saw used here. It makes light work of the project and is simple to use.

Planning your time

DAY ONE
AM: Paint the motifs onto larger tiles; varnish and "antique" tiles

PM: Tile above the fireplace

DAY TWO
AM: Grout; cut and assemble pieces for pediment

PM: Fix pediment to wall; paint

Tools and materials

Ceramic paints

Cornice adhesive

Miter saw

Wooden plate shelves

Ogee (S-shaped) molding

Dowel

⅜" (9 mm) thick particle board

Hot-glue gun and glue

Nails and hammer

Small, patterned tiles

Larger, plain tiles

Barley twist edging tiles

Powder grout

PVA adhesive

Scuffing tool (nails driven through piece of scrap wood)

Clean cloths

Paintbrushes

Saw

Ceramic tile cleaner-conditioner

Tracing paper and soft pencil

Tile adhesive

Notched trowel

Ivory eggshell paint

Antiquing varnish and compatible crackle glaze

Black oil paint

Ocher and burnt umber universal stains

Day One

Step 1
Prepare the tiles using cleaner-conditioner, following the manufacturer's directions precisely.

Step 2
Using tracing paper and a soft pencil, transfer the design from the Template on page 78 onto the tile. To achieve a more handmade effect, make some of the lines more uneven than others.

Step 3
Paint the design onto the tile with an artist's paintbrush. Repeat the conditioning, transferring, and painting on another large tile. Follow the manufacturer's directions for setting the paint to harden. Many ceramic paints are cold set, but some need to be fired in a domestic oven to solidify. Varnish and "antique" the painted tiles when set by adding a two-part crackle glaze following the manufacturer's instructions. Accentuate the crackles by rubbing dark oil paint into them. "Antique" the new Delft-style tiles to match in similar fashion.

Step 4
Roughly lay out the tiles above the fireplace to assess the final spacing and best placement of the motifs. Mark out just inside the area to be tiled to guide adhesive application.

Step 5
Using a scuffing tool, roughen the surface of the wall. Seal with a solution of 1 part PVA adhesive and 1 part water to ensure reliable adhesion.

1

2

3

4

5

6

7

8

9

Step 6

Using a notched spreader, spread tile adhesive onto the wall approximately ⅛" (3mm) deep. Apply tiles, using a twisting movement on each tile to embed it squarely and firmly. Allow to dry for several hours or overnight.

Day Two

Step 7

Mix PVA adhesive with water in a ratio of approximately 1 part PVA to 5 parts water and color this mixture with ocher and burnt umber universal stains. Use this water to make up the powder grout to a dryish, mud-pie consistency. Apply carefully with a brush and remove the excess grout gently with a soft cloth.

Step 8

Using a miter saw, cut the plate shelves to the desired angle for the pediment, remembering that the angles in a triangle total 180°. Cut to length and nail them to form a triangle, making sure that the plate groove is on the outside of the triangle. Place this on the particle board. Draw around inside the triangle and cut the particle board to size using a regular saw.

Step 9

Place the particle board triangle inside the triangle border until it is level with the plate groove. Nail the two together. Using a glue gun, put dowel in place to conceal the plate groove and provide texture. Miter cut ogee molding, and using the glue gun, attach it onto the particle board triangle for a classical look. Attach to the wall with cornice adhesive and paint with ivory eggshell paint.

Further decorative ideas for tiles

You could even use pressed flowers in a design like this, which will not need to withstand frequent contact with water. Simply protect with two or more coats of clear spray varnish. Forget-me-nots at the corners of a tile would give a charming trompe l'oeil Delft-like effect.

Glossary

Miter saw

Notched trowel

Caulking gun

Acrylic gold size
Glue to affix metal leaf.

Aggregate
Gravel and/or coarse sand that is mixed with cement to make concrete.

Caulking gun
This is used for applying certain glues and sealers accurately.

Ceramic paint
Available from craft stores in a myriad colors in either cold-set or heat-set varieties. Both types will set hard on ceramic tiles if properly prepared according to the paint manufacturer's instructions.

Cleaner-conditioner
Product sold alongside small cans of ceramic paint that is applied to tiles to provide a clean, secure key, or rough surface, for good adhesion.

Coarse sand
Coarse-textured sand that is mixed with cement to make concrete.

Cotton swabs
Useful for cleaning fussy areas or removing paint splashes; also for placing small pieces of mosaic.

Craft knife
Extremely sharp knife used for precision cutting.

Dowel
A length of round wood having a small diameter.

Dust mask
Mask that covers nose and mouth to prevent dust inhalation.

Epoxy adhesive
Strong, two-part thermosetting glue that can bind most materials.

Expandable sponge
Compressed sponge that is easy to draw a design on when dry, but that expands to form a painting stamp when placed in water.

Goggles
Essential protection for eyes when nipping tiles.

Grout-removing tool
Tool available from hardware stores used to rake out grout from joints between tiles.

Hydrochloric acid
Acid used for cleaning cement scum from a finished mosaic. It is sold diluted from hardware stores. Always wear goggles and gloves when using and rinse the mosaic liberally with fresh water after use.

Metal leaf
Thin metal sheets used in gilding.

Miter saw
Saw with selectable fixed angles and support to cut mitered joints.

Notched trowel
Spreader that makes it simple to apply a uniformly thick bed of adhesive for perfectly flat tiling.

Particle board
Smooth board made of glue and sawdust.

Powder grout
Cement-based dry powder that, when mixed with water, produces a strong, matte grout. Also available in a frostproof formula.

PVA (polyvinyl acetate) adhesive
A white water-based glue that gives a strong bond. Also available in a waterproof version. Watered down, it can be used as a sealer. When dry, it gives a clear finish. PVA is available from hardware stores.

Scouring pads (non-metallic)
Used to remove excess grout from virtually flat mosaic surfaces.

Scuffing tool
Homemade tool comprising nails driven through a piece of scrap wood. Used to roughen surfaces so that tile adhesive will bind well.

Shellac
Gold-colored varnish used to seal metal leaf to stop it from tarnishing.

Smalti
Handmade mosaic pieces of irregular size and texture.

Stencil brush
Stiff, short-bristled brush used in this book for cleaning fussy areas in mosaic projects after grouting, particularly those involving awkwardly shaped objects.

Tessera (ae)
Generic term used to describe individual component of a mosaic; literally—tile (and tiles).

Tile adhesive
Adhesive used for sticking tiles to a surface. Waterproof tile adhesive is also available for projects requiring frequent contact or total immersion in water. Both are available from hardware and craft stores.

Tile nippers
Spring-loaded pincers for trimming tiles and china to size.

Tile saw
Carbide-bladed saw for cutting awkward shapes in tiles and china.

Tile squeegee
Soft, rubber-bladed tool perfect for spreading and cleaning grout on smooth, flat surfaces.

Tongue depressors
Inexpensive wooden spatulas available at drugstores. Useful, flexible, perfectly clean and smooth disposable spreaders for both tile adhesive and grout.

Universal stains
Inexpensive colors that may be used to custom-tint many kinds of paint, as well as the water used to mix up powder grout.

Wooden skewers
Small wooden sticks useful for placing small pieces of mosaic.

Tile squeegee

Tongue depressors

Tile nippers

Templates

Gilded window recess

A B C D
E F G H
I J K L
M N O P
Q R S T
U V W X
Y Z

Pictoribus atque poetis. Quidibet
audendi semper fuit aequa
potestas. Scimus, et hanc veniam
petimusque damasque vicissim Pictoribus
atque poetis. Quidibet audendi semper
fuit aequa potestas. Scimus, et hanc
veniam petimusque damusque vicissim.
Pictoribus atque poetis. Quidibet audendi
semper fuit aequa potestas. Scimus, et
hanc veniam petimusque damusque vicissim

Templates

Daisy mosaic table

Templates

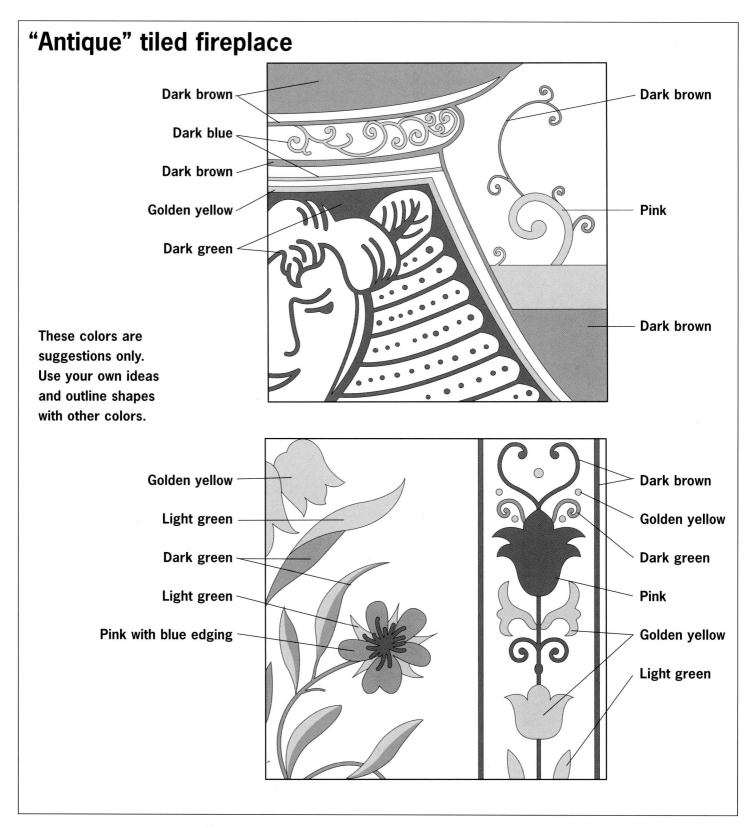

"Antique" tiled fireplace

Dark brown

Dark blue

Dark brown

Golden yellow

Dark green

Dark brown

Pink

Dark brown

These colors are suggestions only. Use your own ideas and outline shapes with other colors.

Golden yellow

Light green

Dark green

Light green

Pink with blue edging

Dark brown

Golden yellow

Dark green

Pink

Golden yellow

Light green

Suppliers

MAIL ORDER MOSAIC SUPPLIERS

Art Glass Source
P.O. Box 4104
Clifton Park, NY 12605
Toll free: (800) 405-6363
Fax: (518) 371-9423
www.artglass-source.com
Mosaic tiles, glass, grout, stepping stone molds, glass cutters, lamp kits, mosaic table bases, and more. Call for a complete catalog.

Fleetwood Building Block
240 W. Main Street
Fleetwood, PA 19522
Tel: (610) 944-8385
Fax: (610) 944-0827
www.fleetwoodblock.com
/fieldbed2.htm
Sells 50lb (20kg) bags of 1–3" (2.5–7.5cm) pebbles in plum, emerald, roseate, and black.

Mendel's
1556 Haight Street
San Francisco, CA 94117
Tel: (415) 621-1287
Fax: (415) 621-6587
www.mendels.com
An art and craft supply store with a large selection of mosaic glass, tiles, and tools.

Mountaintop Mosaic
P.O. Box 653
Castleton, VT 05735-0653
Toll free: (800) 564-4980
Fax: (802) 468-2183
www.mountaintopmosaics.com
Supplier of vitreous glass, smalti, mosaic tiles, and tools.

Stroke of Genius
2326 Fillmore Street
San Francisco, CA 94115
Tel: (415) 776-2529
Fax: (415) 776-2543
Carries vitreous glass tesserae, cut stained glass, glass gems, broken ceramic tile, tools, adhesive, grout, and accessories. Call for a complete catalog.

MOSAIC INFORMATION

Mosaic Matters
www.asm.dircon.co.uk
This "online magazine for all things mosaic" offers feature articles about mosaics, exhibitions, how-to tips, listings of workshops, and a Q&A section.

GENERAL CRAFT

Hobby Lobby
7707 SW 44th Street
Oklahoma City, OK 73179
Tel: (405) 745-1100
www.hobbylobby.com

Michaels Arts & Crafts
8000 Bent Branch Drive
Irving, TX 75063
Tel: (214) 409-1300
www.michaels.com

Zim's Crafts, Inc.
4370 South 300 West
Salt Lake City, UT 84107
Toll free: (800) 453-6420
Tel: (801) 268-2505
Fax: (801) 268-9859
www.zimscrafts.com

GENERAL ART SUPPLIES

Jo-Ann Fabrics and Crafts
www.joann.com
(website includes store locator)
Store questions: (888) 739-4120

HARDWARE/ HOME IMPROVEMENT STORES

Home Depot U.S.A., Inc.
2455 Paces Ferry Road
Atlanta, GA 30339-4024
Tel: (770) 433-8211
www.homedepot.com

Lowe's Home Improvement Warehouse
Customer Care (ICS7)
Lowe's Companies, Inc.
P.O. Box 1111
North Wilkesboro, NC 28656
Toll free: (800) 44-LOWES
www.lowes.com

PAINT PRODUCTS

Delta Technical Coatings
2550 Pellissier Place
Whittier, CA 90601
Toll free: (800) 423-4135
Fax: (562) 695-5157
www.deltacrafts.com
Acrylic, glass, and fabric paints.

EK Success
P.O. Box 1141
Clifton, NJ 07014-1141
Toll free: (800) 524-1349
success@eksuccess.com
www.eksuccess.com
Paints and general craft products.

Index